Winetasting's Magical Moments

Winetasting's Magical Moments

My Most Transcendent Experiences in Forty Years as a Consumer

by

Donald D. Joye

ISBN 13: 978-1-105-25661-5

Preface

The wine world has grown rapidly in the last twenty-five years. Large corporations and smaller, artisanal winemakers have succeeded in matching their product to the taste and desires of the marketplace. Wine is now more popular than ever and is produced all over the world. Plenty of books describe these regions and their wares. They are readily available in bookstores and over the internet. Most are written by wine professionals, expert in their fields. Wine has a huge variety in taste, style, quality, and price. It's not a quick read, but rather a lifelong study.

Wine has been an intimate companion of humanity since the days of Noah thousands of years ago. Since biblical times wine has been a subject of discussion, from moral warnings about overindulgence to encouragements about the clear, healthful benefits, and social conviviality that brighten man's days on the earth.

It doesn't take much to make wine. It happens naturally. The yeasts are right on the grape skin at the moment of ripeness. All it takes is a little juice, and the process begins. Yet, making great wine is not easy. It takes knowledge, dedication, care, and skill. And, speaking relatively, only a few winemakers do it. These great wines, however, transcend the mere consumption of a liquid. It's all about taste, flavor components, texture, and the match with food. It is here that wine shines like no other beverage. It is here that the dining experience can be elevating and satisfying beyond mere physical pleasure. It is here that wine attaches itself to the human soul.

In this narrative, even though it is nonfiction, I have chosen to write in a third person literary style using my alter ego, Carl Beckett. I relate my best experiences in forty years of wine drinking as a consumer, not as a person in the wine trade. As such, all my purchases were made in wine stores, with the attendant cost and risk. So choices had to be made between cost, quality, and region. Of course, I was guided by wine writers. My tastes developed over the years, as would be a common experience with consistent wine drinkers. All wines were tasted in a meal context, not a wine tasting and spitting routine, as the wine gurus need to do. After all, it is work for them. Consequently, the food and wine pairing affects the experience, but wine is meant to be tasted in that context. So the experiences I describe herein are not merely objective tasting notes or wine ratings by the numbers, although all of the wines described are mostly legendary 90+ point or above wines, save one or two disappointments. I focus here on the subjective experience of tasting wine—that experience that lifts the soul, that opens new worlds of wonderful discovery, that are epiphanies of the mind and the taste buds. Most of these wines would qualify for that Rabelaisian quote about Montrachet, "It should be drunk bareheaded and kneeling."

I chose to lead with the "corks," because that is the first experience in the wine drinking process that is more than just visual. Taste in wine varies widely, and wine drinking is often subjective, but there are recognized producers of excellence, and pretty much everybody knows it. What are the elements they recognize in the wine that make it stand out among its peers? What makes for all-time great and memorable wine tasting experiences? I describe here the varied outstanding experiences I have had over the years that have made me an enthusiast for the world of wine.

Not every wine that comes out of the bottle is an outstanding experience, nor does it have to be. Most wine is pretty satisfying for what people want in an accompaniment to a nice dinner. Some wines are flawed. And some are...well, fabulous, almost an otherworldly experience. Is that what makes wine so fascinating for humanity? Some wines are oftentimes more than the sum of their parts. Poets wax eloquent over them. Wine gurus speak in hushed tones and rate them 100 points, or something close to that. I would call such moments transcendent, epiphanies, moments where new realities of pleasure and satisfaction come into being, awakenings (yes, plural), that await the sensitive and discerning wine drinker. "*A votre santé!*" as the French say. To your health—spiritual as well as physical. Read on and enjoy!

The Whites

Chapter One

The drawer gave a low, swooshing sound as Carl opened it—carefully and slowly. It was almost full of a most unusual artifact—wine corks. Carl was a wine lover and had saved not only the labels, at least the ones he could get off the bottle, but also the corks. He did not know what to do with them. But sometime in the future, an idea would arise, he was sure. And so the corks went into the drawer—awaiting the bright idea of another day. Trivet pads, wall displays, whatever.

"Ah, yes," he mused, as his fingers lifted one of the corks from the collection, "*the 1985 Laville Haut-Brion. I remember this one.*"

He twisted the cork in his fingers, observing the imprint—the name, the year, the chateau—and gave it a little squeeze. It was still firm. "One of the greatest white wines I ever tasted. Incredible, perfect."

His memory went back to the time he had drunk the wine. He had expected it to be a great wine, though at the time, he did not know what that meant. It had cost him a hundred dollars, quite a chunk in that day. But not all expensive wines were great. He had bought it on recommendation of Robert Parker, the wine guru, not the mystery writer. It had sat in the cellar for ten years. He had drunk it on its fifteenth birthday.

"The wine needed time," Parker had said. And he had followed that sage advice. He opened it, not knowing exactly what to expect, but at the first sip, a symphony of flavor and nuance greeted him. He had drunk white Bordeaux before, but nothing like this. The wine was bone dry, as expected, and it did not have the tangy acidity or fruitiness of so many white wines. But it had amazing body and extract. A vinous character rather than fruity, this was an aged wine after all. But the flavor and the harmony stunned him.

"Waxy," Parker had said.

He hadn't known what that meant, but he did now. It *was* "waxy"—but not unpleasant. Not unpleasant at all. It was waxy in a way that added to the body and the flavor. A seamless component, beautifully integrated. This neutral element made the wine blend with food superbly. In fact, it made the dining experience altogether different—elevated— almost divine. The chicken with cream sauce was a perfect foil, a superb match. And the dinner and the wine played off against each other. But the wine lingered in his taste buds, in his awareness, in his imagination...and in his soul.

He sipped it by itself.

"This wine is incredible," he exclaimed, "never tasted anything like it. As good as Montrachet...maybe better." Le Montrachet was reputed to be the greatest dry white wine in the world. But Laville Haut-Brion was one of the world's greatest white wines, too.

He tried to identify the components so he could write his impressions down in the cellar book, the way he kept track of all the wines he had drunk—the good and the bad, the mediocre and the outstanding, the great values and the duds. It was the only way to make some sense of the huge, somewhat intimidating, and certainly fiendishly complex world of wine.

The cork was still in good condition, and almost twenty years old now. He remembered what he had written about the wine.

"First time for a Laville Haut-Brion. Always wanted to try one of these." This was not a wine one drank every day. This was something special, a rare, expensive treat—one of those lifetime experiences. He had written, "Nice, complex, smooth, deep, nuanced, dry, has aroma, balance, some oak still. Well-integrated, pleasing with no flaws. Mellow, well aged. Excellent." Aping the Parker rating system, he had given it a "98"—essentially perfection. Parker had given it a "93"; the *Wine Spectator* a "95."

The label had always fascinated him, too. The twin crosses at the top spoke of St. Andrew and St. George, though the chateau was in France, not England. It was in the Bordeaux region—almost right inside the city of Bordeaux. It was an ancient property. Had it been owned by the church at some time? Could that have been the reason for the crosses? Or did they come from the time in the 1300s when the English ruled Bordeaux?

"Appelation Graves Contrôlée," the label said. And right below it—"Cru classé"—classified growth. This was a wine of superb pedigree. Below that was the year—1985. And then the owners, "Domaine Clarence Dillon S.A." It was American owned. Clarence Dillon was the United States Secretary of the Treasury in the 1960s, and he had always remembered that signature on the dollar bills he had handled in those days—*C. Douglas Dillon*. Strange what the mind retains. Clarence had passed away, but his offspring still owned the chateau. So there was always that connection. He felt that it was, at least, still part American. And about that, he was strangely pleased.

The Dillon family had owned the great first growth red wine, Haut-Brion, for fifty years. And recently, they had bought their cross street rival, La Mission Haut-Brion. Laville Haut-Brion, the sister property, had also come with the deal. La Mission Haut-Brion—perhaps that's where the crosses came from.

"So this is why they write poetry about wine," he mused, swirling the golden liquid in the glass. "This is amazing. It won't go away. The flavors persist, grow, and interact, like an orchestra with all the instruments playing. And it's all going through my head—but wait, something else ..." He put down the glass and thought for a bit.

There was something profoundly *satisfying* about this wine, something right. Something beyond the facts and figures—the coldhearted realities of quantitative measure—the color, the dryness, the elements of flavor and character.

"It sings," he mused. "This is really good. Really good. Time after time."

In a world of stress and conflict, here was peace. In a world of falsehood and mediocrity, here was excellence and truth. In a world of anxiety, disappointment, and frustration, here was satisfaction—amazing satisfaction, surprising satisfaction. In a world of twisted ugliness, here was beauty, surpassing beauty. In a world of dullness and the ordinary, here…was transcendence. Quiet, not flashy or dramatic. Not advertising itself, but being itself, transparent. The real thing, as if the Creator put it there for mere mortals to stumble across and reflect on the wonders of life. And there it was—sitting in the glass. He swirled it again.

Here was something one could taste, experience, and not merely know about. One could engage it, live it. One could take another sip, if something was found to be elusive. The discovery was endless, fascinating, like learning at the feet of a master teacher. Awe inspiring.

How do they make stuff like this? he thought. *How is it possible?*

It *was* an outstanding vintage year. That was part of it. Parker had said it was one of the three best in the last twenty years. There was no doubt about *that* in his mind, though this was the only Laville Haut-Brion he had ever tasted.

"Are they ordinary mortals, the ones who made this wine?" He wondered. Would they think of it as highly as he? Would they strive to make another like it? How could a mixture of grapes, Sauvignon Blanc and Semillon, age this well and give this flavor and character? He wondered if he could afford to taste anything like this again, but he purposed to try. Someday, somehow, he would return to this.

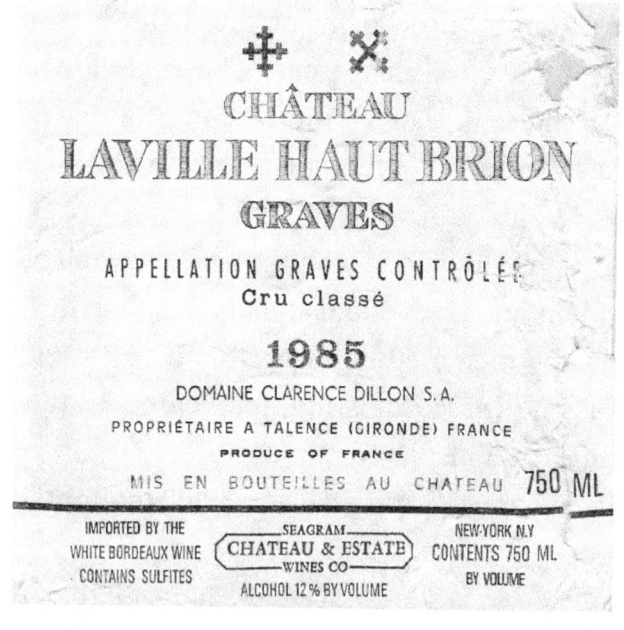

As a modern note, the name of Laville Haut-Brion has been changed to La Mission Haut-Brion Blanc by the new owners. Winemaking, like any business, is constantly changing.

Chapter Two

Carl's hand reached into the drawer again. A smaller, shorter cork emerged. Schloss Johannisberger 1964—a Cabinet level wine. This was a German white wine made from the Riesling grape. They called it Grünlack, or green capsule. It was for the table, for food.

"Yes, this," he said quietly. It had been a fabulous wine, but he hadn't tasted anything approaching this since that time. "Why can't the Germans make wine like this again?" Because of that blasted law of 1971, a law that turned German winemaking into something resembling painting by the numbers. You could dump all the wine of Germany into one huge tank and sell it for ten dollars a bottle. It would taste fine, as German wine is usually well made, but it would have lost its sense of identity, of individuality, of something really special. He doubted he would taste a Riesling like that one again from Germany. But what a loss!

The wine was the best German Riesling he had ever tasted, and he had tasted quite a few. It was almost dry, "off-dry" they called it. It had substance and extract, a perfect balance of elements that made the wine almost mythical in proportion. Slight acidity, but one hardly noticed it. The total harmony was what one noticed. That and the extract, the flavor, the impression it made.

"Man, this is really good wine," he observed. The flavors went on and on. There was a depth to the wine, almost indescribable. A slight austerity, but mollified by the unctuous extract—a sign of perfectly ripened grapes.

The wine had just disappeared into his taste buds, leaving behind a wealth of impressions, all subtle, but firm, definite, substantial. Not like some ghost or mere apparition. No, the wine had weight, but it wasn't heavy at all. A medium body, he recollected. Not thick, not watery either.

The history of the estate went back to AD 800 and Charlemagne, whom the Germans called "Karl der Grosse"— Charles the Great—the tall, blond, athletic, and intelligent German warrior and statesman, who, with leaders of the church, had founded Christendom—a European, Christian civilization in the wake of three hundred years of warring, wandering German tribes that history calls the Dark Ages. In doing so, he fulfilled the vision of the great Augustine, Bishop of Hippo Regia, a Roman and the most influential saintly writer of the first millennium. Charlemagne had noticed that the snows melted first on the hills of this section of the Rhine River, and he caused vineyards to be planted there.

The label was an unusual one. Ornate. A pink banner announced the one-time owners—"Fürst von Metternich" and family. This was the same Metternich who presided at the peace conference of the Napoleonic wars. The Austrian mayor of Vienna, who, after assisting Beethoven in his legal struggles surrounding his nephew, Karl, never received the promised work from the hands of the great master. He had been given this estate in the Rheingau, a wine growing region of Germany, after the war. The family descendants had held it ever since.

Aristocratic. Yes, it had an aristocratic aura about it.

"But why haven't they made anything as good since?" The question haunted him. The wine had been so excellent. He had bought subsequent bottles of the same year. They all tasted the same—consistently well made; no bottle variation. It had been a wonderful experience.

The food he had tried it with had been varied. It had gone well with chicken dishes especially. In fact, it had been perfection with chicken. But he had also drunk it with *Sauerbraten*—a German beef dish. It had been excellent with that also. Perhaps the slight sweetness in the sauce of that dish had made the white wine bridge the gap for a red meat dish. But it had also gone well with fish. It hadn't overpowered the fish, the subtlety of the wine working a wonder with such meals.

He shook his head. "What an amazing, versatile wine this was. Why can't they make more like this?"

He reached into the box again. Out came a cork that said, "Chateau Grillet, 1967."

"Oh, yes," he recalled, "here's another one-time transport to heavenly realms." This was the best white wine he had ever tasted in a dry, Chardonnay style. But it wasn't Chardonnay or white Burgundy; it was a Rhone wine made from the Viognier grape. The property had its own appellation and microclimate, tucked right into a hollow along the mighty Rhone river of France, between Lyon and Avignon.

"Another famous property that can't seem to duplicate the excellence of this wine," he thought. "This was utterly fabulous." And a totally different experience, yet in its own way just as superb and satisfying as the Schloss Johannisberger. How can excellence in wine take on so many dimensions?

The wine was a medium golden color. He had aged it for eight years or so. It's not something usually done with wines of this type, but Chateau Grillet was different, made to age. The years had just gone by, just "happened." He had opened it out of curiosity, but the wine had come recommended, and it had pedigree. He had paid a high price for it and expected something special.

The aroma was quite fruity and noticeable. It reminded him of jasmine flowers, or honeysuckle. But the taste of the wine was utterly different. Not a hint of sweetness. It was bone dry—really bone dry. The driest wine he had ever tasted. But it had intensity, simmering intensity. And focus. Never had he experienced a wine with such laser-like focus. And like all great wines, it had substance, flavor, a dimension of depth, and a complexity totally unique. It was a little austere, but warm at the same time. The fruit tasted fresh, grapey, like the aroma suggested, but the wine was totally devoid of sugar or sweetness or unctuousness. It was neither angular nor sharp, but rather mellow in a taut way, subtle, but not light. It had plenty of complexity, depth, and flavor. It was so intense, it seemed to vibrate with life—a characteristic that was translated to the drinker.

"I really liked this," he recalled. The style was so interesting—an incredible combination of what seemed like opposites. Yet, the harmony was stunning, the intensity arresting. The alcohol was hardly noticeable. It had been a superb match with chicken and cream sauce. Phenomenal! The sharp focus of the wine cut through the richness of the dish, and the flavors melded together almost magically.

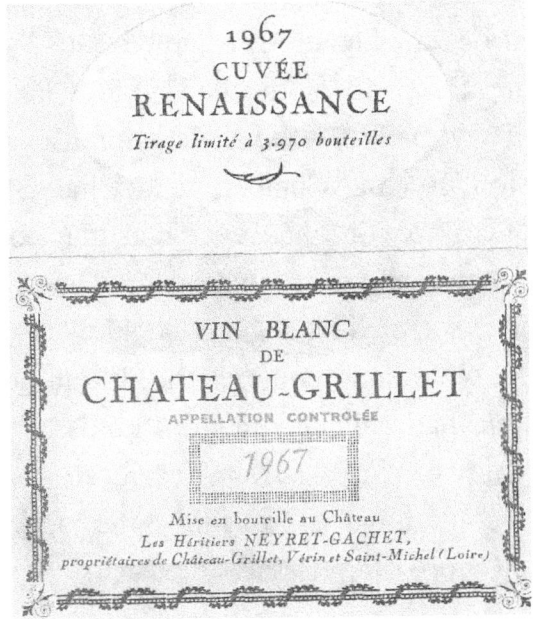

"Another transcendent experience. I'll remember this one forever." But they had not been able to reproduce it since that time. Had the estate relaxed its quality standards? Had they become lax with success? Had greatness become a bore to them, with the wine selling itself no matter what they did? Was it just the vintage year—a freak of nature never to be repeated again? Even wine writers had noticed the fall in quality over the years and had not been shy about discussing that in public. Modern Chateau Grillet is a very fine wine, make no mistake about it, but it generally lacks the greatness it once exhibited— as in Carl's 1967 bottle.

"When will I ever taste another one like this?"

Some white Burgundies of the 1985/1986 vintages had come close. They had that bone-dry, intense richness, and flavor dimension. But the Chateau Grillet had been mythical. In his experience, no wine had ever had that combination of flowery fruit, intense and dry richness, and laser-like focus that made the wine seem like it was making a statement to humanity, to all who could comprehend. It had been a riveting combination, and had enhanced certain kinds of food in ways he had never known or met before. It had elevated the dining experience to something approaching the divine. And one could only want more of the same.

Chapter Three

"Ahh, where is that Mondavi Chardonnay?" Carl rustled in the box looking for a special cork. It was a 1990 Robert Mondavi Chardonnay Reserve—the best California Chardonnay he had ever tasted. Other Mondavi's had been good, but lacked the special quality of this wine.

"Sappy and rich in vanillin from the oak," he recollected. "Must have been the bottom of the cask or something." The vanillin had been so pronounced, but the combination was delicious. He had tasted hints of this in a white Burgundy some years before, and it had made an impression in the brain.

Sometimes California Chardonnays could be too rich, a little overwhelming and too fat—not enough room for flavor dimension. Other styles were too lean, too citrusy, too oaky, or had a petrol or gasoline overtone that was not pleasant. But this Mondavi was a classic. Something about it had arrested his attention, making it memorable.

"Ah, here it is," he exclaimed quietly, as he held the cork between his fingers. "This was nice."

The wine was golden in color with a medium to full body, dry, but not too dry, nicely extracted, and well-balanced between all the elements—fruit, depth, flavor, and acidity. But it was the vanillin that had caught his attention. Not overdone, not harsh, not off-flavored—a perfect marriage of the wine and the wood, with a little extra. No wonder they put this kind of wine in oak.

Few people, alive or dead, did more for California wine than Robert Mondavi. Winegrower, winemaker, wine seller, wine advocate, member of many wine societies, and still active into his eighties—an incredible life in wine. And he had great achievements, which included foreign interests in leading collaborations: with Baron Philippe Rothschild of Chateau Mouton in Bordeaux as they developed the Opus One brand together, with others in Italy, here and there. The Mondavi Cabernet Reserve was often one of the better California Cabs. And the Chardonnay Reserve was also highly regarded and well respected.

Persistent enthusiasm was what set Robert Mondavi apart. That and the entrepreneurship—the constant appearance before the public and the steady and vigorous involvement in all the happenings in California wine. Largely due to his efforts, others were encouraged to try their hand at wine making in California. The results speak for themselves. California is now a world-class wine making area—for red as well as white wines. The climate seems to favor Cabernet Sauvignon for reds and Chardonnay for whites, but other grape varieties also grow well there. As winemakers refine their craft, the wines get better and better.

He thought about the food matches with this wine. Fish was too mild for it. It needed a substantial dish, chicken with some kind of sauce. The rich cream sauce was especially good. He smiled. Chardonnays were not mild wines. They were bold, substantial, and flavorful. Not delicate, shy, or light.

On the other hand, there was a wine that was delicate, shy, and light. It was superb, too. But it had been developed by a Japanese winemaker for sushi—a very subtle and delicately flavored dish. Since Carl had developed a recent taste for sushi, he had been fascinated to try the wine. It was called "Oroya" and seemed, at first, to have been made in Japan. But it was not. It was made in Spain, using a few Spanish white wine varieties, by a Japanese team. It was not a wine to lay down, but rather one to be consumed early, so it had a plastic cork, and he had not saved it.

The wine was lightly colored, a faint yellow gold, and light to medium bodied. It had noticeable fruit and was dry, but not bone-dry or intense. It was subtle, with an interplay of flavors. And the acidity, though noticeable, was light—just enough to keep the wine fresh and vibrant.

What an achievement, he thought, amazed. *And what a novelty—a wine developed specifically for food!* Usually it was the other way around. You had to find the food that suited the wine. What an ingenious idea these Japanese had come up with. And quite a successful one at that.

Well, what wine *does* one serve with sushi? He had often eaten the typical Oceanside combo, as they called it—a mixture of tuna and salmon sushi rolls. He had also bought a tray of *nigiri*, sushi with a slice of the raw fish right on top of the rice without being rolled up in a *nori* seaweed sheet. He had also tried a vegetable roll with just the thinnest slice of raw salmon in it.

The meal gave very subtle, delicate flavors—not unpleasant. And one did have to watch out for the pungent and spicy wasabi, a potent Japanese horseradish variety that is commonly used as a condiment with sushi. But ordinary wine would be too strong, overpowering this dish. He had actually thought about this problem before. What could one really serve with sushi? Tea went well, but he was thinking of wine. A German Riesling would be too sweet, a Chardonnay, too strong and flavored. Perhaps a New Zealand Sauvignon Blanc would do—maybe. He had tried one. It was good, but had a little too much cut and was a little too dry.

But the Oroya was perfect. It was amazing that a wine could be developed for a specific food. They had used three grape varieties. The back label explained it—one for flavor, one for subtlety, and one for fruity aroma and for making the wine taste a little off-dry, not too harsh or intense. One of the grapes was to compliment the spicy wasabi. They had succeeded beautifully, and it was only ten dollars a bottle. A superb achievement!

Satisfying wine is not always about price or small, limited, and hard-to-find production.

Chapter Four

"Now, where did that Trockenbeerenauslese cork go?"

Carl rummaged through the box again, searching for the cork that had sealed a bottle of the magical German sweet wine made from "botrytised" or moldy grapes harvested very late in the season. This special mold let water escape through the grape skin and concentrated the sugars and elements within the grape. It lent a mild flavor to the wine, not unpleasant. Only in certain years when conditions were ripe for the mold to grow—foggy mornings and damp days—could this wine be made. The wine was highly concentrated in both extract and sugar. And after fermentation, quite a bit of residual sugar was left, hence, the wine tasted very sweet.

It was a delicacy—a golden nectar—an amazing feat of nature shaped by the skill of the winemaker. This was the height of German wine making. One should sip it slowly in order to taste all the flavor elements. It was not really a wine for food, but rather one to drink by itself.

He had compared it to the famous Chateau d'Yquem of France, which is made in much the same way, only with different grapes—not Riesling. In fact, many grape varieties could be used to make similar wine. But the Riesling had such subtle nuances and depth of flavor, that the others seemed almost crude by comparison. The d'Yquem had been wonderful, too, but he thought it had been opened too soon. With age, it would have had much more nuance, like the Trockenbeerenauslese. The German word stands for special picking of dry berries. The grapes are not totally dry, but have reduced water content due to the action of the botrytis.

The wine was quite sweet, but not cloying. The sweetness had other elements to balance that out. It had a "raisiny" component, but that did not dominate. It was unctuous and thick from the glycerin in the wine, but not too much. It had a slight acidity component that kept the wine fresh and vibrant— not dull or flat. The concentration of flavor was amazing—a totally unique tasting experience. The wine would have interfered with most dessert dishes and was meant to be drunk by itself *as* the dessert. It had enough substance to hold one's attention, as the flavors enveloped one's taste buds and continued to leave an impression in the aftertaste. What an amazing experience.

The color was bright and clear yellowish gold with brownish overtones, almost a coppery sheen. One could see the viscosity of the liquid as one swirled it in the glass. The d'Yquem had been much more yellow, golden in color.

The wine was a Hochheimer Domdechaney 1964 vintage. A Rheingau wine made not too far from the Schloss Johannisberg, in a larger sense between Bingen and

Frankfurt/Main. The wine was made by Schloss Schönborn in Hattenheim. An ornate coat of arms filled the left side of the label with two lions carrying Austrian and Imperial German flags. The label itself had a light tan/yellow background with the inscriptions in black, red, and gold. The label, bordered in old gold and red, has changed little in fifty years. Other sweet wines he had tasted did not hold a candle to this.

Carl's hand rustled in the cork drawer again. "Ah, this cork belongs to one of the most classy and well-known properties in all of German winedom," he exclaimed. This was the Bernkasteler Doktor vineyard from the Wwe. H. Thanisch estate in Bernkastel on the Moselle (the Germans spell it "Mosel") River in the hills, west of the Rhine in Germany, north and a little west of Bingen. The Romans had established a major settlement at Trier, on the southern end of the Moselle River, and even at that time had known of the wines. There was a famous and ancient song about Moselle wines—"Oh, Mosel-la, yes, you have so much wine ... do you drink the wines alone?" (It rhymes in German).

Bernkastel is part of the Mittelmosel, or the mid part of the river, halfway between Trier and the Rhine, where the best wine is reputed to be made. The Doktor vineyard is probably the most famous in Germany. All of the vineyards are steep, hillside slopes, but with excellent sun exposure and protection from the wind. The climate is favorable, but the terrain makes harvesting an arduous task.

The 2004 Moselles were touted by the wine press—the Kabinetts in particular. The *Kabinett* designation refers to the first quality picking of the vineyard. These wines are generally lighter and drier than the later Spätlese or Auslese, etc., pickings, which are fuller and sweeter. Carl now preferred his Rieslings on the drier side and so was interested in trying a few. The Thanisch wines he was familiar with from past experiences, and they were not cheap. But given the overall cost of fine wines, they were a relative bargain, and so he bought one.

Five years after the vintage date, he opened it—and what a surprise! German wine did not need lots of aging time, although it could stand ten years or so. Four to six years was perfect. Carl's notes read, "Classic Moselle. Light green gold color, light/medium body, light acid/light sugar balance (this is the critical factor for German wines), has fruit, complexity, glycerin, impeccable class, and harmony—sappy and vinous with classic grapey aftertaste. Super! Sorry I drank it."

After five years, it had disappeared from the marketplace, and he couldn't get another. Ah, frustration in wine! An all too frequent occurrence. If we could only know ahead of time, Carl thought, a more satisfying and economical wine buying experience could be brought into being. "I suppose that's why people go to the winery, so they can taste ahead of time," Carl mused. But these wines were made thousands of miles away across an ocean, and so, that is regrettably impossible. And one can only do the best one can.

The label was also a classic. On a white background, the hills, vineyards, and the town by the river's edge were portrayed in brown. The vineyard's name, written in gold, was at the top in banner style. There were two "c's" instead of "k's" in the name nowadays. The label was bordered by a green band with a gold thread in the middle and gold vine leaves at the corners. Below the vineyard's name was the vintage date in black. And below that in larger, red type were the grape variety (Riesling) and the harvest level (Kabinett). Below the central picture of the hills and town was the estate bottling designation in black-on-white. And below that was the producer information in a gold banner with vine leaf filigree on the sides. The label was attractive and eye-catching without being garish. Like the wine, it reeked of class and style.

Carl's hand rustled in the cork drawer again. "Ah, this cork belongs to another one of the most beautiful and classy properties in all of German winedom," he exclaimed. This was from the Scharzhofberg estate in Wiltingen on the Saar, a tributary of the Moselle in the more southerly part of the river.

The Scharzhof is one of the most beautiful and well-situated estates in Germany. It sits in a hollow among the hills surrounded by green vineyards. It survived undestroyed through several wars—WW II being the most recent and terrible. It has been in the hands of the Müller family for hundreds of years.

The wine was the most delicate, flavorful, steely, fruity, and complex Riesling—a wonderful Riesling with that lightly tart and faintly sweet combination in a light bodied elixir that only the Moselle can produce. In the right year, it was absolutely unique and perfect as this one was—a 1964 Spätlese. The 1990 came pretty close.

"At last, a wine up to the reputation of Egon Müller," he exclaimed at the first tasting. These wines were well-known and highly respected in the trade and also by wine writers and critics. He had tasted several of these wines of different vintages before and had been disappointed. Too acidic, too sweet, not the fine balance he expected, etc. etc. This region only gets one or two perfect vintages in a decade. But when it hits, the result is nectar of the gods. And that's what it reminded him of. It was almost a sacrilege to have it with food! The wine was so delicate, so sheer, so alluring and feminine, so diaphanous. He could not but think of heavenly things—angelic beings, Greek goddesses around the throne of Zeus…. It was light, but not insubstantial. It seemed to pass through his senses, through his head, and into his soul. Something resonated there, just the slightest ruffle, yet it aroused him to dreamy reveries.

"This was really something."

He had had several others since that one experience. And the wines had all possessed a unique, classy style, but the price had gone up, and the availability had gone down, so that he hardly saw it anymore in the marketplace.

"What a pity that not more of this is available."

When it was on, there was no other Riesling in the world that could compare. It reeked of class and superb wine-making and made an indelible impression on the memory.

The label was one of the most distinctive, artistic, and beautiful in all winedom. On a white background, a flowing black script slanting upwards and to the right describes the estate and the wine style. The year was just above the end, and below, in a finer, smaller gold script, was the owner and the estate bottling notation. A few curls and swirls fill the lower right. Filling in the upper left corner was a picture of the estate house in a subtle gray-green nestled in a valley of the Saar River with long, sloping hills covered in vines. An ornate vine in gold leaf separates the view of the estate from the rest of the label. A few grand prizes were noted in small gold print at the lower left of the picture. At the top, set off by fine gold lines, was the other necessary information—the importer, the grape, the region, the country of origin, and the type of wine. Other essential information from the wine law of 1971 was at the bottom in small, black print. The tasteful, multicolored label had been a delight for the eye for decades. Elegant excellence.

What a wonderful tradition. Carl hoped they would never change it.

Donald D. Joye

Chapter Five

Sometimes great wine can be a surprise. The 2002 André Bonhomme, Viré Clessé came into Carl's recollection immediately. The wine had been written up in a restaurant review in the newspaper, and Carl had decided to hunt it down. The Bonhomme whites were the "house wine" of a very famous Philadelphia restaurant, and they had mentioned in the article how good the 2002 was. So Carl had to try it.

It was more than good. His scrapbook entry read, "light yellow-gold color, medium body, one sip and you can tell this is really good wine; impeccable balance, has some extract, flavor, complexity, and harmony. Dry, medium/low acids." He had given it 92 points, but in the light of later experience, perhaps he should have rated it higher and bought some more!

Years later, he sought more of the same in later vintages. The store personnel consistently and uniformly mumbled something about the present vintage being good, but not quite the 2002. It had made such an impression on everyone.

Viré Clessé is loosely classified as a white Burgundy because it is Chardonnay, but it grows in a region closer to the Beaujolais wine district, a bit further south, the Mâconnais. Hence, its wines are reasonably priced. White wines from the

Mâconnais are notable values, and they generate a fair amount of interest in the marketplace. The Bonhomme has a reputation for making clean, consistently good wines—that's why it's a favorite at top restaurants.

But the 2002 was special. Everybody knew it. What makes a wine of a given vintage so special? A lot of people would like to know the secret of that. Who can explain it? Sun, rain, or lack of same? Place? Vinification technique? The barrels? It is one of the most delicious but maddening conundrums in wine. Sometimes…it just happens. Had Carl only known earlier, he would have bought a lot more. Alas, knowledge comes oftentimes too late.

The label was a model of classy simplicity. On a background of bone, off-white, the appellation "Viré Clessé" stood out in gold cap script in the center. Below it, in green, was listed the producer. The label had a three-ringed border, and the essential information—type, volume, alcohol content, etc.—was tastefully displayed in small print here and there. The year was handled by the neck label.

It was no wonder at all that this was a favorite at the first-class restaurant in the city.

Not all great wine was tasted in the USA! Carl remembered the trip he had taken to England years ago, and what a surprise awaited him in the southern English coast near Hastings—the Carr Taylor winery. He had read about it in the "sites to see" brochure provided by the conference organizers, and it had tripped his fancy. So he went on a winery tour, in England no less, and sampled.

The Carr Taylor winery was one of the better known wine producers in England. It is located in the southeastern corner of Great Britain, where, they say, the climate is quite conducive for growing fruit. At the tasting, Carl noticed that they made a quite decent dry white table wine that was pleasant and food-friendly. Then they got to the sparkling wines.

Carl was blown off his seat almost at the first tasting. Whoa! This was a big surprise. The sparkling wine was excellent—probably the best nonvintage champagne-type wine he had ever tasted. It was stunning. This had the mouth feel, flavor, and class of high-level French champagnes. He tasted both the regular and the rosé, and they both had the same wonderful character. He bought a few bottles to take home, but in retrospect, he should have bought more. Who could believe that English sparkling wine could be this good?

A few years later, Carl revisited the two bottles he had bought in England. The notes were consistent with his past experience. "Excellent champagne," he had written. "Has flavor, depth, balance, medium acids, nice aroma, off-dry, has substance, tasty." He could have added—"all you want in a great champagne" and "for a very modest cost." He couldn't get enough of it. Pity they don't export. Perhaps someone should convince them to do so!

The label was plain, yet dramatic, predominantly black with a gold edge and a coat of arms at the top center. The essential information was provided in starkly contrasting white, with "Carr Taylor" prominently displayed in the center and "Medium Dry" above it and "Quality Sparkling Wine" below it. A little English understatement there, it seemed to Carl.

What makes great champagne? Carl thought of all the champagnes he had known in forty years of wine tasting. There were only a few memorable ones and almost all of them were high-level French champagnes costing upwards of $100 per bottle. There were, thankfully, a few modestly priced champagnes—or sparkling wines as they must be called on the label if they are not from the Champagne region of France— and of these the Carr Taylor was clearly the best. The substance, depth, and flavor dimension, the great balance between low acids and low sugar, the fine harmony, and just the right amount of "fizz" distinguished it from the others in its class. And the aroma was a nice touch.

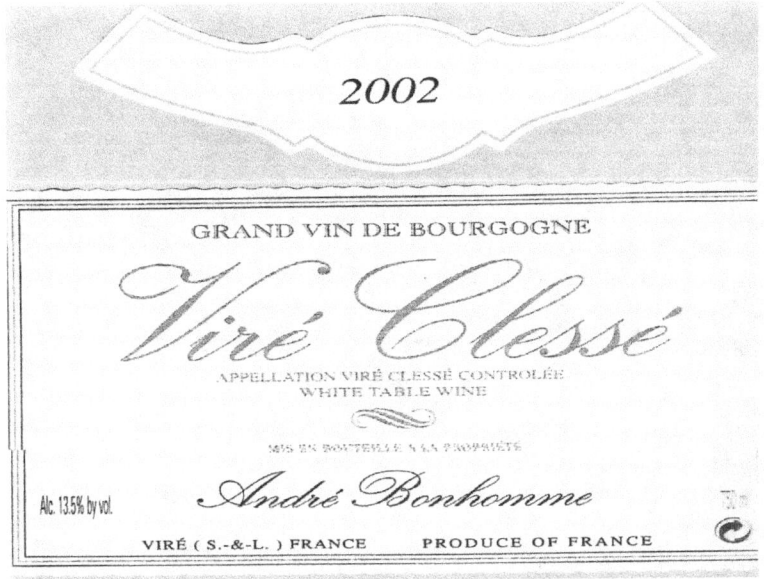

The Reds

Chapter Six

Not every wine Carl had tasted was tasted in solitude. Carl was a member of a dinner group that often had wine tasting with a meal. He smiled as he recalled his friend Bob's comments at one of those dinners. They had tasted two great Bordeaux, the 1983 Chateau Lafite Rothschild and the 1985 Chateau Haut Brion, among a few others, at that meal. He had preferred the Lafite for its richness and depth, but Bob had commented often, "This is really good" about the Haut Brion. He had said it quietly and seriously, swirling the liquid in the glass with something that approached real respect. Bob, a New York attorney at one of the prestigious law firms, was to be believed because he had actually lived for a decade in Bordeaux, spoke fluent French, and had learned about the wines there first hand. Bob's experience had authenticity, so Carl had listened carefully.

"What is it about the Haut Brion that makes you say that?" he had queried Bob. He had not gotten an analysis in return. Only the same quote repeated in the same way. At first it had annoyed him, but subsequently, he had sharpened his analytical skills and sought, with more concentration, the key to the mystery of Bob's comment in the wine itself.

The wine was lighter than the Lafite—not as rich or immediately engaging. But it had subtlety and an unusual lightness for a red wine. It was from a vintage characterized by that, but somehow the lightness was not a fault, rather it was buried in the character of the wine. It was simply charming. But the complexity snuck up on him. Given a chance, the layers of flavor and character could be discerned. The harmony was also very apparent. It was an effortless wine—not demanding, not heavy, not weighty—but, oh, so good! And so satisfying. The more one looked, the more one found.

There was no element out of balance. The wine hung together seamlessly. The flavor was fruity, grapey, but not sweet, though the impression was of sweetness—or perhaps ripeness. The texture was firm, not rich or unctuous. It was more transparent rather than opaque, a lady more than a blockbuster. The tannins were nicely mellowed out. Yet, there were flavor elements, somehow not exactly definable, that made the wine a riveting success. No flaws, no hard edges. The impressions did not come on right away. They grew with each sip. It was really amazing. The wine could speak, if one had the ears to hear! It was a thoroughly enjoyable wine and easy on the senses.

He had to agree with Bob. This was indeed "really good wine."

Amazing, sometimes, what one can learn in the company of others at a shared meal with wine.

"Ah, what have we here?" Carl murmured, as he took a long but somewhat shriveled cork out of the drawer. "Chateau Cheval Blanc, 1955," it said.

"Ah, yes. This is the one we had with the T's—almost by mistake. What a wonderful wine this turned out to be."

One year after that vintage, the Cheval Blanc property experienced a devastating frost that killed all but a few of their vines. They had to start all over again and didn't produce much high quality wine for some time thereafter—very small productions in both the 1959 and 1961 vintages in Bordeaux— two of the greatest in the region's long and storied history. As a result, the Chateau missed out economically as well. It took real dedication and hard work to get the property back on track.

Something about the Cheval Blanc had touched a chord in Carl's psyche. What was it? The flavor was different than most Bordeaux. It was made from primarily equal parts Cabernet Franc and Merlot. No other chateau used this much Cabernet Franc. There was no Cabernet Sauvignon, the primary grape variety in Bordeaux. None at all. Is that what made it different? Wine writers often commented on this. Cheval Blanc was the greatest place in the world for Cabernet Franc—usually a secondary grape in the rest of Bordeaux. And Cheval Blanc had made one of the greatest wines ever in 1947—a mythical wine that wine writers and experienced professionals still speak of in hushed and longing tones.

But Carl did not find the grape variety argument altogether persuasive. The flavor *was* a little different, he acknowledged. But he liked it. It wasn't grapey, neither bold nor flashy. Something about the wine said "subtle substance," and the more one tasted, the more one was drawn in. He noted briefly that the wine had made a good impression on his guests, but they were not used to drinking wine, let alone fine wine. And though they enjoyed and appreciated the wine, the true greatness was not really apparent to them.

The wine had class and breed—almost indefinable and not quite tasted. Felt, maybe. It was something like an "umami" component, a subtle truffle-like presence that just added to the weight and complexity of the tasting experience. The wine was seamless, no hard edges, flavorful, and smooth. No jangling acids to notice; no harsh, bitter, or puckery tannins to detract. No off-flavors or mold or other obvious wine flaws. But the wine had a subtle substance. This was not the greatest of vintages of the '50s, but Cheval Blanc had made a magical wine. It was fifteen years old when he opened the bottle. Time enough for all things to mellow and meld together.

The wine was medium-bodied, not full or overly rich. But the substance was there. The flavor dimension was there. The depth was there. The harmony and the mellowness were there. One came back to it time and again. Mmmmmmm. That was all one could say.

"This...*this* I like!"

The label was a little old-fashioned, with lots of curlicues. There were the gold medals the property had won at world's fairs in Paris and London prominently displayed—one on the left and one on the right. The title "Chateau Cheval Blanc" was placed as a curved banner in "old gold" ink over the rest of the details on the white-background label. The year and "St. Emilion" was written below the title. And both of these were flanked by the gold medals. Cheval Blanc—the white horse. Don't all the heroes ride white horses?

And so, Cheval Blanc became one of Carl's favorite wines. He bought other vintages and drank them when they were ready, but not all were like this one. Some were, and some weren't. The '83 was superb, for example. Carl gave it 100 points. "All that you want in great Bordeaux," he had written. "Coming back for more and more. Super." The '85 was nice also, but didn't have the outstanding character of the other two. The wine experience can be a fleeting thing, but with Cheval Blanc, as with other famous great wines with pedigree and a track record, one could depend on a repeat performance—

maybe not always—each vintage is different. Every year the winemaker has to prove himself, and now often, herself, again. But commitment to making great wine year after year is an achievable, if arduous, goal, and many talented people seem to be up to the task.

Donald D. Joye

Chapter Seven

Can the Italians make wine? Can the Italians make wine!

No, no, I mean great wine—like Bordeaux. Well, they haven't tried—not until about thirty years ago.

The 1983 Sammarco, Carl remembered, was one of the wines of pedigree in Italy. He had placed the cork in a trivet, along with others, to make a hot plate or serving pad, or to hang on the wall if that suited him.

The label was smaller than most and declared up top on a quasi-octagonal shape "Castello dei Rampolla." The estate makes several top wines of which "Sammarco" is one of the flagship labels. A stylized coat of arms and a drawing of the castle sat below the estate name and above the "Sammarco" name. Then the details of origin, etc., follow in small print below the name. In larger print in gold at the bottom was "Vino da Tavola Toscano." This was an interesting designation because, by Italian wine law, only Sangiovese and related grapes can be used for red wine in this Tuscan region. And Sammarco was Cabernet Sauvignon. So what the Italian producers of fine Cabernet in the region have done was to label their wines above as "table wine of Tuscany." The legality of authenticity was denied, but the quality was in the bottle. And it's reflected in the marketplace pricing.

The Sammarco had dark medium color, subtle and fine aroma, medium body and nice richness. It was smooth and mellow with good Cabernet character and only slight puckery tannins. It was consumed eleven years from the vintage date. The wine had very nice and noticeable balance and harmony with an interesting flavor component, something like mint. It had nice, well integrated complexity, and was superbly drinkable and a great food match, blending into the meal and adding subtly to the whole experience. Wonderful. Wines like this give a little something to life, something pleasing, satisfying, and enjoyable. No wonder people pay for it.

There was another, very unusual Italian wine that Carl had found intriguing. He was attracted to the reputation first, then the distinctive blue/brown label second. "Castello di Fonterutoli, Siepi 1996." Hmmmmmm, a Sangiovese/Merlot blend sounded interesting. So, he bought it. Oh, yes, it was recommended by the wine salesman, a supposed expert on Italian wine. He had no reason to doubt him, and Carl was curious. It was expensive, but not exorbitant. It would sit in the cellar, waiting for an appropriate time to be uncorked.

That time came eleven years after the vintage date at a dinner Carl had for guests. The guests were wine familiar, but not wine sophisticates, and he thought they might like the Merlot part. As he poured the wine into the glasses at the seating arrangements for the guests, he noticed the deep, dark color of the wine—almost like a young Bordeaux of a great vintage. Very dark color, black-purple, almost opaque.

At the dinner, the guests enjoyed the wine immensely. And so did Carl. A little surprise, he thought. The wine was delicious with no hard edges. Perfumed and fruity, it went down easily and was a great match with the food—a beef dish with some excellent brown sauce from a first-class local restaurant. It had aged nicely and had good flavor dimension. But there was something more to this wine than mere enjoyment, though that was there aplenty. The wine had an Italian lightness and gaiety about it. An immediate, uncomplicated pleasure.

"Hey, this is really good," several of the guests commented.

But underneath, where most of the guests overlooked or did not taste carefully enough, Carl noticed quietly, was depth—nuance, richness and complexity—lots of it. Layered and harmonious and beautifully balanced, as if the Sangiovese and Merlot were singing to each other, each touting its own strengths. No jagged edges, no flaws, no discord, or dominance of one element over the other. The Sangiovese, with a slightly austere bite and that unique flavor that makes Tuscan wine so popular. The Merlot with that delightful smoothness and substance which magnificently fill the holes left by the

Sangiovese, added a rich fatness to the wine and a delicious flavor component that makes great Merlot almost catnip in the marketplace.

The wine had come from a great vintage, and the ripeness could be tasted and sensed in the wine. It was like a symphony of flavors going on and on, or more like a concerto grosso in the style of Handel, Vivaldi, and the other great Italian masters—one group of instruments playing against the other in masterful counterpoint. Or like watching Ginger Rogers and Fred Astaire move across the dance floor, or that astonishing couple, Torvill and Dean, skate-dancing on ice with flawless movement and expressive motion. This was wine that could be called the Petrus of Italy. Chateau Petrus is the legendary wine from Pomerol—that small area of Bordeaux where Merlot reigns supreme and gives wines of delicious fatness, ripeness, and texture that emerge in great years. And it fetches great prices too; after all, the whole world knows it…and wants it.

"Terrific wine! Buy more," concluded Carl's notes. A "95" rating.

The Italian climate can ripen Merlot wonderfully. Great Italian winemakers are starting to take advantage of that, and the blend with Sangiovese is being explored. This has potential for world-class, first-class wine. There is a Pomerol in Italy, waiting to be discovered, developed, and sold to a world just itching to be pleased in this way.

Italy has many wine growing regions, not just Tuscany. The other famous region for Italian wine is in the north—the piedmont or "Piemonte" in Italian. These are the foothills to the Alps, and the climate is generally cooler than farther south. Here the grape of choice is the Nebbiolo, which is a delicate grape variety like Pinot Noir. Everything has to be right, and only then can great wine be made. Huge technological advances have been made in this region in the last twenty years. The Nebbiolo makes two slightly different kinds of wines in different regions—the Barolo and the Barbaresco. Carl had sampled both and had come to have a slight preference for the Barbaresco. But when the Barolo is good, it is outstanding and unique.

One such Barolo was the Giacomo Conterno, Barolo Cascina Francia, one of the estate's top wines. Carl remembered how the 1990 was a near perfect example of such a wine. "Best Barolo ever tasted," said his notes. Red fruits, not harsh, some licorice and caramel, medium body, some fruity acids still, lighter styled wine full of nuance. Some mellowness from the age (it was drunk about fifteen years after the vintage), not too much power, good food match." He had given it a "95." Parker had rated it the same.

The label had reddish brown band spanning the top and announcing the producer. The word "Barolo" was in the center in black script superimposed over a coat of arms. Below this in smaller print was the location, "Cascina Francia" and other details. The neck label supplied the year of the vintage.

This was not Carl's favorite style of wine, but he had to marvel at the excellence of it. How the character of the wine showed through, with all the elements mellowed with age. And they were easy to pick out and ruminate upon. It was a demonstration, a lesson, of what fine wine should be all about. A "tour de force" Parker would say.

CONTERNO

BAROLO

DENOMINAZIONE DI ORIGINE CONTROLLATA E GARANTITA

Cascina Francia - Serralunga d'Alba

DRY RED WINE
ESTATE BOTTLED BY AZIENDA VITIVINICOLA
GIACOMO CONTERNO di GIOVANNI CONTERNO
MONFORTE D'ALBA - PIEMONTE - ITALIA

NET CONTENTS 750 ML.   PRODUCT OF ITALY   ALCOHOL 14% BY VO

Chapter Eight

Ah, Burgundy! That rogue of wine tasting—the gorgeous, elusive, alluring, seductive, mysterious, and finicky mistress of love. One thing out of whack and the suitor is left at the door dreaming. One missed cue, one awkward hesitation, and she drops you. Say the wrong thing once, and she is gone. No second chances. Such is the lady of Pinot Noir. Everything must be right to make great Burgundy. With a northerly location and iffy weather, the challenge is substantial.

Yet, there is something in this wine on occasion, some chemical that reaches the deepest centers of the brain that are wired for pleasure and ecstasy. All of us who have experienced it know it. Try to repeat it! It's almost impossible.

Burgundy can be the most frustrating wine in the world, not because it is bad wine. But only because it does not, perhaps cannot, consistently deliver the once known taste of heavenly glories. But we come back, time and time again, assiduously seeking that experience of ecstasy. Ever reaching, ever searching, till we perhaps find it once more, in all its fullness—or lacking that, some facsimile of it, some semblance, some ethereal whiff of wine paradise. But it happens all too rarely. Is it some deviousness in human nature or just the way life is that we should prize the most what we can have the least?

Carl's thoughts went back to the days he was a young professor and had attended a technical conference in Washington, DC. The day had been long, and he had met his former advisor there, along with several other graduate students. After the conference that day, they had all decided to go to a restaurant in DC for dinner. It was one of the smaller restaurants, and the service was slow. Carl was asked to choose the wine. With so many different people there, it seemed best to pick a wine that he thought might have broad appeal.

He asked the steward for some recommendations and got three. He picked the Burgundy—the Courcel, Pommard Epenots 1966.

When the food was ready, they came around with the wine. They had ordered only two bottles, since most of them did not drink wine regularly and would only sip it. The waiter opened the bottles and went through the wine ritual with Carl.

He sniffed the cork. It was fine. "Okay," he said. But the aroma was enticing. Was it because they were famished and his senses were tremendously poised? That whiff, just a sweet, vinous aroma, carried with it the promise of character and rich flavor, a brief, heart pounding second of anticipation.

The waiter poured the glass. The wine was the brightest red color he had ever seen in a wine. Like the paint job on a bright red Ferrari, or *The Graduate*'s Alfa Romeo. It had clarity, depth, and shimmering brightness. Most wine was much darker, sometimes opaque. Not this one. Clear as a bell. Bright red. Something special was coming up.

He put the glass to his lips, sniffed, and took a sip. Incredible. Even today, he could remember, if only faintly, the deliciousness of that wine, all of its nuances wafting through his head. It was only six years old, but a perfect age for that kind of Burgundy. The wine had a wonderful fruity flavor— subtle raspberry, light strawberry, a little rich cherry/berry mixed in, and a ripe, sweet impression, though the wine was dry. But it also had depth, presence (not so much power, but substance and extract) of essence—that sappy "vinousness" that is a major turn-on for all lovers of fine wine. It was all wrapped together seamlessly with the laser-like fruit in a total, perfectly balanced, harmonious package.

It was medium bodied with a smoothness that reminded him of whipped cream. An incredible texture he had never encountered at that time and rarely met since. It was not oily or overly unctuous, but it had…what does one say? Velvet, something like velvet. He could not get enough of it. It totally arrested his attention like no other. He treasured every sip and slowed the meal as much as possible to get all the ecstasy he could. It seemed to vibrate in his soul as if it were alive, coursing through the brain paths of ecstasy. The God of the universe was speaking to him through it, and he was riveted in rapt attention.

At the end of the meal, he took the empty bottle home along with the cork. The label was a simple design with a thin red and green border enclosing the pertinent information. The wine was from southern Burgundy, the Cote de Beaune, where the wines are generally lighter, fruity, and don't last as long as those from the more northerly parts. Pommard was noted for flavorful wines, but they did not have, as a rule, the elegance or the polish of this one.

He bought every wine of this type and producer he could get his hands on. They were good, but not the special character of the '66.

And so, eventually, the wine became a memory—a cherished one to be sure, but one that had not repeated itself all the rest of Carl's years. He always remembered it with a pang of longing, as if this had been his one great love—lost years ago—with all the epiphany, passion, hope, and dreams that had gone with it.

There was another style of Burgundy that had also impressed him. This was more typical of the northern regions of the Burgundy wine area. Grands Echezeaux—one of the

Grand Crus of Vosne Romanée. This was the '64 made by Joseph Drouhin, a well-known wine negociant even today.

He had bought this on a whim. It was the first grand cru burgundy he had tasted. In the book *Wines* by Julian Street, the site had been written up quite favorably, and so he gave it a try.

The wine was dark reddish colored, more in keeping with normal wine color. It was more full-bodied and more obviously rich and complex, with a firm, forward flavor and character. It was almost "meaty" in a good sense. If it did not arrest the senses the way the Pommard had, it was subtler, yet quite substantial and flavorful, a thicker, more chocolate-y wine. The fruit could not be discerned quite so easily. Raspberry and currants came the closest, but the flavor was distinct, clear and delicious.

He had tried the wine for no special occasion, just a simple meal and an exploratory gustatory experience. The wine had been expensive, but...this *was* wine tasting, after all. One had to pay the price for high-quality experiences.

There were no hard edges to the wine. It was about seven years old and beautifully integrated and harmonious. It was superbly balanced, with rich nuances and a deep, dark impression to it all. It did not shout; it was subtle, and yet substantial, with a kind of presence of a strong friend coming alongside, and giving support in the face of some threat. This was the darker, richer, earthier style of Burgundy from the Cote de Nuits. Nowadays, this is the style most emulated in Burgundy, a style driven primarily by wine critics. It is, of course, delicious and wonderful when done right. But the lighter style of Burgundy also had its considerable charms.

There are other places in the world in which good Pinot Noir can be found. For example, Oregon, California (finally, in the northern, cool climate areas) and New Zealand—but they are all developing sites without a track record or "terroir" delineation. Burgundy is the capital of Pinot Noir, and has been for hundreds of years. It is rarely equaled for great Pinot Noir. All of the great sites in Burgundy are well-known and well described in the wine literature. Every year the wine gurus report on the vintage for Burgundy fans around the world.

1966
POMMARD
Grand Clos des "Epenots"

APPELLATION CONTROLÉE

Mise en bouteilles au Domaine

DOMAINE DE MADAME BERNARD DE COURCEL
POMMARD, COTE-D'OR, FRANCE

Joseph Drouhin

BURGUNDY RED TABLE WINE   PRODUCE OF FRANCE   CONTENTS : 12 FLUID OZS.

GRANDS-ECHEZEAUX

APPELLATION CONTROLÉE

MIS EN BOUTEILLE PAR
JOSEPH DROUHIN
Maison fondée en 1880
NÉGOCIANT A BEAUNE, COTE-D'OR
AUX CELLIERS DES ROIS DE FRANCE ET DES DUCS DE BOURGOGNE

SOLE AGENT *Dreyfus, Ashby & Co* NEW-YORK, N. Y.

Chapter Nine

"Ahhh, here's an oldie," exclaimed Carl as he drew out of the box a gnarled, almost shriveled cork—Portuguese Garrafeira. "Eight bucks a bottle twenty some-odd years ago." One of Stan's favorite wines. He had spent some summers with his brother, Stan, in Baltimore. Stan had taken him around to the local wine shops, and they had tasted a number of inexpensive wines to fit both their budgets. The Portuguese wine was one of Stan's favorites, and he agreed it was good.

Stan was an amateur chef, could have been professional, but choices are made in life, and life goes on. The deal with his wife, Kathy, was that she would rarely do the cooking, but would do the clean-up afterwards. Cleaning up from Stan's cooking was no small task, but she didn't mind because the dinners were so good. Stan's dishes were always unique and some of them classic. Carl and Stan had enjoyed many an hour discussing wine and food.

What fascinated them both, and something they found true in both Portuguese and Spanish wines, was the unusual affinity the Tempranillo, or Tinto, grape had with tomato sauce dishes.

"Spanish wine goes better with Italian (tomato sauce) dishes than Italian wine," they both exclaimed at different times. What is it that happens between the two? All too few wines ever showed that synergy, and it happened so often as to become wine lore with them. This, even though a young Chianti of a great vintage could be occasionally superb with spaghetti—its freshness and flavor beautifully matching the tomato sauce in the dish.

But for Carl, the Pesquera Tinto, a Spanish wine, in a good vintage was his favorite. It had a little more body and flavor than the others, aged well and generally had that "magic" with tomato sauce dishes—chicken parmesan, spaghetti, lasagna, pasta with tomato sauce, and other Italian dishes of like composition.

Twenty years ago, Spain was a relatively backward region for wine. The traditional wines were made, and they were good, if you had a taste for them. But they were not in an international style. The comment was often made that if Spain ever woke up, the world of wine would gain a major player. The climate in Spain is generally dry and hot, somewhat similar to California and Australia. Certain grape varieties flourish in such climates—Tinto and Garnacha (Grenache) especially.

In recent years, mostly due to the EU policies and standards, Spain has awakened from a long sleep. It is now one of the hottest producers of wines of all price points in the marketplace. Yes, they still produce inexpensive, good red wine of the type Stan and Carl had enjoyed, but they also produce some very high-end wines that compete with the best in the world, the most famous and most mysterious being the legendary Vega Sicilia Unico.

The Vega Sicilia is a Cabernet—grown in Spain and carefully vinified and aged in a great Spanish tradition. The wine is expensive and rare, but Carl had always wanted to try it. It needed age, so one had to be patient.

Finally, the day came. Carl had bought the 1976, a decent year, and had drunk it twenty-two years later. The wine was relatively light in body and color, not uncommon or unexpected for wines of this type from northern Spain near the Rioja region. The wine was very mellow and subtle with faint tannins and a sweet impression, though the wine was totally dry. It had a unique flavor with a very nice vanillin component from the time it spent in barrel. This was an older style Spanish red and had a mellow, lighter character than most Cabernets. One would be hard pressed to recognize it as a Cabernet. It was an elegant, graceful style with a significant mellow wood component that was pleasant and different. And of course, many people liked it, including Carl, who rated it a "95."

The label, like that of Penfolds Grange, was heavy on text. At the top, "Vino Fino" in large letters identified it as a premium wine. The coat of arms followed below, then the large "Vega Sicilia" name with the year and the type of wine below that—Unico—all in plain black script on a light, off-white, bone-colored background. Below that in fine print was a listing of the many honors the wine had won over the years and around the world. Then a box contained the vintage details and the bottle number. Written below that was the region, the importers, etc.

At one time, Vega Sicilia was the only internationally recognized first-growth wine of Spain, but nowadays the stores are full of first-class Spanish wines, and the wine gurus are singing their praises. There are many styles to choose from. Spain has arrived as a world-class wine-producing country.

In one of the newer efforts in winemaking, the Pesquera group has broken new ground and created a wine like Pesquera, but a little more favorably priced for the marketplace—Condado de Haza. This is in the Ribera del Duero region in Spain, directly abutting the Rioja region in the north. The 2001 vintage in Spain had been highly touted by the wine press, and Carl had decided to try the wine.

The label was dramatic and colorful in the Pesquera style. What appears to be a painting of the view of a small Spanish town in bright sun and clear blue sky serves as the background of the label—the houses in light tan stone and red-orange tile roofs. Centered in the label and below is the wine "Condado de Haza" in stylized black and in strong contrast to the background—suggesting shade perhaps. Below that in white on a black band and in smaller type is the listing of the necessary information about the producer, the alcohol content, the volume, etc. The vintage date and the region designation are in the upper right corner. The "Pesquera" designation is in the upper left corner.

This was typical Spanish Tinto wine. Carl's notes read, "Dark, clear reddish color, vinous perfume, warm attack, good harmony, medium/full body, light acidity, well-integrated Tinto flavor dimension, good with food—nice beef match, has power and presence but no hard edges. Faint tannins. Buy more!" The wine was six years old when Carl drank it with steak—92 points. Parker had rated it 91 points. The price was $20. Another terrific wine value. But it was the flavor dimension that grabbed Carl's attention. Delicious.

Chapter Ten

Ah, California! Carl had several corks of fine wines from that world-class region. But the 1994 Caymus, Special Selection, had impressed him the most. Other vintages of this wine were frequently up to the same quality. The 1991, for example, was almost just as outstanding.

"Can't believe Cabernet Sauvignon can taste like that," he muttered every time he thought about it. The wine was dark purplish opaque. It had chocolate richness without a hint of tannic edge. Big fruit bomb, Robert Parker would say. But the wine also had texture, depth, and body. Beautiful, absolutely gorgeously balanced like a big, fat, lingering, voluptuous kiss. Sweet!

"Wow! I would buy more of this in a heartbeat."

The wine had an approachability normally reserved for Merlot, but there was no Merlot in the wine. It had a deliciousness almost never encountered in wine tasting. One could almost not get enough of it. Yes, this was a very good year in California, and wines from that vintage had a special harmony and fruit not normally encountered. But the Caymus Special Selection had no harsh edges—no sharp tannins, no alcoholic punch, no coarseness or high acidity or off-flavors. The balance was impeccable. All of the elements constituted a harmonious whole in a style that simply arrested one's attention. One could only call it delicious and seductive.

This was not wine to age long; this was wine to drink early and enjoy totally. Surprisingly, the wine went well with food. Some rich and flavorful wines need certain kinds of foods to blend well. Too much flavor in the wine and too much flavor in the food may not make a good match. But this wine "married well" as they say—a wonderful counterpoint to red meat dishes with or without sauce.

The label was subtle and elegant in keeping with the wine's reputation. A unique, light green pastel background showcased the gold appliqué rendition of hanging grapes and leaves on a horizontal vine trellis. "Caymus Vineyards" was written at the top in large print announcing the producer. Below the vines, the year and the type of wine, "Special Selection," were written in a tasteful red script. Then "Napa Valley" and "Cabernet Sauvignon" were placed at the bottom in a bluish-green print. The whole was framed by a green and gold border in a vertical, oblong shape with the corners cut out in a circular "bite." Below the label in black background was the essential information—the producer, location, alcohol content, and the signatures, in red, of the Wagners (father and son) who made the wine. And proudly, at the bottom, was written "Product of USA."

Everyone deserves a shot at this wine, once in their lives, Carl thought. No wonder this is a highly sought after wine. Fabulous. Does the country proud.

Like California and Spain, Australia has arrived in the world of wine. Astonishing successes have come one after the other in the last twenty years in that country. The 1982 Penfolds Grange had always been on Carl's mind, since first hearing of it from Robert Parker. "The only first growth in the southern hemisphere," Parker had put it. Made from the Shiraz grape, it was an homage to the Northern Rhone wines of France, made from the same grape, by winemaker Max Schubert. Nowadays, the wines of Australia have blossomed to great diversity and world renown, so that Penfolds Grange is not the only great wine from that country anymore. But it was, and most assuredly, continues to be, a first-class, first-growth equivalent from down under.

The label was very striking, red text on a gray background, with the title, the vintage, and all the other details spelled out. At one time, it was called "Grange Hermitage" with the homage more specific, but international wine law forced a change to drop the "Hermitage" name as that should refer to the region in France exclusively. So now, it is known just as "Grange." But the wine is stupendous and expensive and needs twenty years to reach its full maturity and give all the subtlety it is capable of.

The '82 was consumed twenty-four years after the vintage date. So Carl had to be patient. The wine was dark and opaque, full bodied and rich. It had an incredibly powerful perfume that, amazingly, absolutely filled the room. It had vibrancy, complexity, and a wonderfully grapey flavor that was fruity but not fresh. One of the guests at the wine tasting commented, "This is really great wine." It routinely scores in the mid-90s from the wine gurus.

The Shiraz grape has very interesting flavor components. It is the fruitiest of the great red wine grapes, and could be the oldest known grape in human history. Evidence of such had been found from diggings in ancient Persia—modern Iran—in recent times. It is a very good hot-climate grape and grows well in California and South Africa, in addition to France and Australia.

Is every bottle of great wine a great experience? Well, it would be nice if that were so. Fortunately, it is, predominantly, but the 1983 major-league Chateau, alas, was not (Let's not embarrass anybody here. Wine problems can happen to anyone). Carl shook his head as he remembered. This wine should have been wonderful, but it wasn't. The cork smelled very slightly of mold—only very slightly. But the wine was spoiled. It tasted severely attenuated, no charm, flavor dimension, depth, nuance, or complexity. It was clearly "off," sour, and sharp. What a great disappointment! Every wine drinker, sooner or later, has an experience like this.

What happened? Was it the cork? This is most often the trouble and has fostered a lively debate in the wine trade about what kind of closure is most reliable. Plastic corks have made their entrance. Screw caps have also. Both seem to work well for short term wines—those meant to be drunk within three to four years. But neither seems suitable for great wines that require long-term aging. Scientific investigations into how a wine ages and the function of oxygen in that aging are being done at a variety of institutions. Closures are being designed with regulated oxygen diffusion in an attempt to simulate what the cork does in aging wine. The science is in its infancy right now, so answers may take time. The wine world is eagerly awaiting the results of those investigations. The *Wine Spectator* reports regularly on such discoveries.

The cork industry has not been idle either. The frequency of bad bottles due to tainted corks has been reduced significantly over the last fifteen years. And the corks are carefully graded, so that the producer has a choice. But better corks cost more money.

Differently manufactured corks are also being used with very good success. These are composite cork midsections capped with a slice of fine, tight, clean cork at both ends. These have worked well for champagne and sparkling wines for many years. Now they are being applied to still wines in the hope of stemming cork taint.

But spoilage may not be due to the cork. Sometimes it is cellar hygiene. Bacteria in the air can enter the bottle during the bottling stage, or get on the cork during storage. Mold can do the same. A myriad of possible catastrophes awaits the winemaker and challenges his or her every act.

Scrupulous cleanliness is a must for the winemaker, and the task is not easy. Considering all the potential disasters confronting the winemaker—from bad weather, to phylloxera beetles eating the roots of the vine, to various molds and vine diseases, to fermentation problems and temperature control, to heat and storage problems, and, finally, the corks. It's a wonder, sometimes, that great wine gets produced at all in the volumes it does. These great winemakers deserve our admiration and respect for the wonderful job they do even if there are occasional hiccups.

And so, his poor '83 Bordeaux was dumped down the drain. It should have been a wonderful experience, and he had paid a considerable price for it. The loss was aggrieving, and he regretted it deeply. But that was life in the wine world— great highs and occasional bitter disappointments. But in wine, as in life, doesn't that reflect the way it is for us all?

The 1961 Chateau Latour was a 100-point wine—all the wine gurus agreed. Carl had bought the wine early in his wine tasting experience on the recommendation of the store owner. He had the bottle, but when should he open it? What special occasion would be complemented by such a wine? Wouldn't everyone interested in wine kill to have a chance to taste a 100-point wine? He could not drink it by himself, all alone, selfishly hoarding such a great experience. No, it had to be shared. A wine tasting dinner would do. And so it happened. Forty-five years after the vintage date, the legendary 1961 Chateau Latour was opened in the company of guests and friends, along with other fine wines.

He was worried about the cork. Would it disintegrate? He was very careful opening the wine. The cork was wet, soaked through, and came apart when he pulled the opener. Slowly, he worked the other bits out of the neck of the bottle. He poured the wine through cheesecloth to remove the last fine bits of the cork and placed the wine in a decanter. He sipped a sample gingerly.

It was good! Thank God. Not sour, not spoiled, not off. It was good. The guests would be pleased indeed.

Chateau Latour in Bordeaux is considered by many to be the greatest red wine in the world. Of course, Carl no longer made such distinctions. Wines from many regions could be as great, and one should not make such tight comparisons. But this Latour was a legendary wine. What would it taste like? Would it be too old?

A thousand anxious questions ran through his mind, but the wine was good, and the dinner should be a great success.

The wine still had dark color. The '61 vintage was famous for dark color—almost black and opaque, concentrated intense flavors, chocolaty character. The wine had the color still, but it was not opaque. It had some acidity still, with medium, rather than full body, but it had retained some of the intensity of the vintage. It had no harsh edges, had aged and mellowed beautifully; it had lots of complexity, subtlety, depth, nuance, and warmth in abundance. In fact, that was the major impression of the wine. One could spend all evening discussing its merits. It had a subtle, leafy flavor component. Tobacco? Olives? It was superb with the food. It just melted, it actually felt that way, into the food—filet mignon tenderloin tips with brown sauce and mushrooms—and elevated the whole gustatory experience. Incredible!

The label was the old style one, with the lion atop the tower, and "Grand Vin de Chateau Latour" in large letters immediately beneath. The newer label is smaller and more Spartan. Beneath the tower of the older label stands the pedigrees: "Premier Grand Cru Classé, Appelation Pauillac Controllée, Pauillac-Medoc," the date, "1961," the chateau bottling expression, "Mis en bouteilles au chateau," and, at the bottom, the proprietors, "Sociète Civile du Vignoble de Chateau Latour." The contents were bordered by a stylized scroll-like outline. The label was a classic, known for almost hundreds of years, and immediately recognized by all cognoscenti of fine wine.

He only thought, *Why didn't I buy more? I could have drunk some earlier and followed the magnificent evolution of such a wine.* Alas, one cannot do everything.

Even though 1961 was the vintage of the century for Bordeaux, the 1982 vintage was, in many people's minds, just as good. Carl had bought a 1982 Chateau Canon because he recollected a previous Chateau Canon being a wine he had liked. The '82 had to be aged, and so Carl waited twenty-seven years after the vintage date to open it. It did not disappoint.

Chateau Canon was a highly rated St. Emilion Bordeaux that had fallen on hard times after the 1982 vintage—cellar contamination. The owners had disclosed this to the public, paid their dues, and were almost ruined in the process. It took committed investors to restore the property to its former glory. However, this took twenty-five years. The cellars and all the wine making equipment had to be trashed. New cellars had to be built, and new equipment bought and installed. Insidious bacteria cannot be dealt with any other way. It was a costly, hard climb back, and those who did it had to have courage and commitment. It appears that the 2009 and 2010 are as good as the 1982, says Robert Parker, and Chateau Canon is back in the high quality wine business.

The label was a little unusual as wine labels go. In a portrait format, Chateau Canon was prominently displayed in cursive script in the center with "St. Emilion, 1er Grand Cru Classe" in a smaller font below it. At the top was a photograph, of all things, of the estate with vines flanking the approach road straight into the chateau. At the bottom, the vintage date, the producer, and other necessary information were listed.

Carl's notes on the 1982 read, "Smooth, harmonious, mellow. The star of the tasting! (It had been tasted in a wine tasting dinner with a group of people). Sweet impression, full body without being chunky, beautiful balance, seamless, wonderful *umami* flavor component that keeps you coming back and savoring the experience. All you want in a very nice Bordeaux. That '82 vintage shines again, 95 points." Parker had given it a "94"; the *Wine Spectator* a "93." Wines like this are immanently satisfying, and in the case of Chateau Canon, reasonably priced given its quality. Carl could only say, "Welcome back, Chateau Canon."

Chapter Eleven

Every treatise on wine must be, out of necessity, incomplete. There is always another vintage. There are always new producers striving for excellence. The wine world is so huge and complex that one cannot taste everything that is produced. Carl had not drunk all the fine wines ever made. He was not part of the trade and did not have such free and unfettered access to the precious bottles. So, there are other fine wines waiting to be experienced, and perhaps there is actually no way to conclude this story. It is, of course, only one man's experience. And such experience is ongoing. As it is for all appreciators of fine wine, the final curtain has not yet fallen. The story is open-ended.

To those who are starting out or whose experience is just beginning, search on. The world of wine is great and inexhaustible. All kinds of experiences await the wine drinker, including the ones just described.

The wine literature is bursting with books on wine written by experienced and knowledgeable people. Some are analytical, some are more descriptive; some are comprehensive, others focus on particular areas producing certain types of wine. Many are newsletters written by trade groups or wine gurus. These are generally reliable sources of guidance for good wine. In addition to the ones used by Carl and mentioned previously, several sources of good information are Steve Tanzer's International Wine Cellar, and the *Wine Enthusiast* magazine, which is particularly good about availability in the marketplace in the Northeast. Allen Meadows's Burghound subscription service is exclusively Burgundy, and one certainly needs some expert guidance to navigate the Burgundy minefield successfully. Alfio Moriconi is known primarily in Europe, but if one finds a wine with his recommendation affixed, it is an almost certainly good wine. In years past, Carl relied on Frank Schoonmaker's recommendations, which were almost always excellent. "Monsieur Henri" was a reliable label for good Bordeaux.

Taken in moderation, matched with food, and made with excellence, wine is a great boon to life here on earth. But it also has deeper repercussions about how life is—as in wine in life. There is a resonance here that no other creation of man can match. Here is an experiential connection with the very forces of life itself that somehow elevate the soul, cause poetry to be written, and cause the Creator to be praised.

Postscript

One might wonder about the other great wines of the world, the ones Carl had not tasted. Some of them are beyond the means of the average consumer, indeed beyond the means of all but the very rich. Romanée Conti and Chateau Petrus can run more than $4,000 per bottle at this point. The first growth Bordeaux, such as Chateau Margaux, Guigal's single vineyard Côte Rôties, and Chave Hermitages run just around or under $1,000, but that is still a serious chunk of money most likely beyond the means of all but the very wealthy. Most of Carl's top wines had been bought before the price explosion. Fortunately, many others have been working hard to fill the gap left by the price escalation of these elite wines, and many fine wines at reasonable prices can be found by those who search for them.

The Wines

1985 Chateau Laville Haut Brion (now known as La Mission Haut Brion Blanc)

1964 Schloss Johannisberger Cabinet

1967 Chateau Grillet

1990 Mondavi, Chardonnay Reserve

2005 Oroya

1964 Schönborn, Hochheimer Domdechaney Trockenbeerenauslese

2004 H. Thanisch, Berncasteler Doctor Kabinett

1964 Scharzhofberger Spätlese (the 1990 was also great)

2002 André Bonhomme, Viré Clessé

NV Carr Taylor Sparkling Wine

1983 Chateau Lafite-Rothschild

1985 Chateau Haut-Brion

1955 Chateau Cheval Blanc (the '83 was also fabulous!)

1983 Castello dei Rampolla, Sammarco

1996 Fonterutoli, Siepi

1990 G. Conterno, Cascina Francia Barolo

1966 Courcel, Pommard Epenots

1964 Drouhin, Grands-Echezaux

1976 Vega Sicilia Unico

2001 Condado de Haza

1994 Caymus, Special Selection (the '91 was also great)

1982 Penfolds, Grange

1961 Chateau Latour

1982 Chateau Canon

THE END